Contents

1 Introduction

1.1 About the Author

I have worked in the Computer Software Industry since the 1980s and seen the industry go through many changes. One of the biggest changes outside of the ever-evolving technology platform was the introduction of Software Testing as a service needed to sit alongside Software Development. This was born as Technology started to get more complex with more options and requirements and interfaces between different platforms, systems and companies. As more people started to use computers and technology there was more emphasis on trying to ensure it worked properly. After many years as a programmer, I moved into software testing and covered System Testing and User Acceptance Testing as I wanted to ensure that when software is delivered it works as you would expect it to.

2 What is UAT?

UAT is User Acceptance Testing. But what does that mean and what is it?

This book is to help explain what UAT is, where it fits into a project and what you might need to do as part of the UAT phase of a project. User Acceptance testing is defined as several things, but it is basically the end user of a system checking to ensure it is fit for purpose and allows them to perform processes to enable them to do their job using the system delivered. This book isn't about explaining the different project management types and software development methodologies, but to help you understand what is involved when you are selected as a User Acceptance Tester.

So how do you know if a system is fit for purpose – first you must define that purpose. This may have been done for you if you buy an off the shelf, prewritten package. Then you need to assess what you will use the system for and try to do your job activities using the system.

If you are part of a project where a system is being written for your company or you are tailoring a package to have additional functionality built for you then you may be more involved in helping to define what the system needs to do to enable you to do your job.

2.1 Why me?

You may have been chosen as you have knowledge of your job that others don't have. You know more about your job, your processes, your customers, what can go wrong with your processes that people in the IT department, the software seller or the Business Analyst.

You might think, there are people whose job it is to test the system to make sure it works, so why do I have to do this as well as my own job. Because you have on the job knowledge. You know how to do your job inside out. You know which customers and processes have oddities that need to be catered for.

2.2 What might be involved in being a User Acceptance Tester?

That depends on the Project, the methodology, the type of software, the size of company, but there are some basic stages that every UAT tester will see in some form or other. You may only be involved in some but it is good to understand them all so you know what to expect.

2.2.1 Requirements Analysis

This where Analysis is done to understand what is required for the business / customer from the system. It might be done as a series of workshops, reviewing business processes and rules or playbacks of what the system does now (as is) to see what changes need to be made (to be). The outcome of this phase could be a number of documents called User Stories, Business requirements, Functional requirements document, Business requirements definition or may just be a spreadsheet with a list of requirements.

Being involved in this stage will help to understand what might need to be tested in UAT as you should be proving that all the business requirements captured have been delivered as expected. Most projects that are delayed are usually because the business requirements have gaps in them that when the system gets tested and you start to use it you realise that something else is needed. Consider this during the business requirements phase and try to assess all situations that might arise later on. They may not be included in the scope of the project but at least they have been considered and assessed at this early stage.

2.2.2 Writing Test Cases

Writing Test cases is the key phase that is often not done thoroughly enough and leads to errors post go live. To write test cases you should review the business requirements and consider real life scenarios that will arise when using the system. Also consider that every test could have an opposite. There are more details in the next section with examples of how to write test cases.

Test cases can be written on an excel spreadsheet or you may be asked to use one of the many testing tools to record your tests. These are generally just a fancy spreadsheet that produces lots of reports and graphs and makes it easier to reuse the tests again in the future. Most tools are straight forward to use but there should be basic training available if you need it.

2.2.3 Data

Data is key to testing and having good data for your tests can reduce the amount of testing that you need. Again, it is good to consider real life data both common data that is used the most and data that you know causes problems. You know your data better than anyone so use your knowledge and experience to make the system better.

2.2.4 Running Tests

Running tests consists of following the test scripts and performing the activity in the system and recording the outcome. Has the test passed or failed? Did it do what you expected it to? It is always good practice to record some details of what you have done, details of the account created, screenshots are always useful to refer back to in case you rerun a test and it is now doing something different. If a test fails, you will usually need to raise a bug to capture what you expected to happen and what actually happened to allow a developer / designer to review the observation and assess if a code change is needed. This phase is also very useful as a training exercise as you get to see the system working before you need to use it in a live scenario.

2.2.5 Reporting

There are usually a lot of reports produced during testing to assess the quality of the system. Numbers of tests run, failed, passed, left to run. Numbers of bugs raised and closed. Time taken to close bugs. Priority and reason for bugs. Reporting should be defined in advance to understand what is needed for the project and also how these are to be produced and by who. You may be responsible for producing these or you may just be the receiver of the report.

3 Requirements Analysis

This often starts with a list of requirements, which are then assessed for things like priority, importance, complexity. This list is then reviewed to provide more details. The list of requirements should also be assessed to see if they are testable.

An example of a list of requirements may be -

Requirement	Requirement Level	MoSCoW	Complexity
1.To be able to place orders on behalf of our customers	1	Must	High
1.1 To select items to place on an order from a specific list of items	2	Must	Med
2. To be able to Create a Customer	1	Must	High
2.1 To be able to capture multiple contacts for a customer	2	Should	Low
2.2 To capture name, delivery address, invoice address, payment methods allowed, telephone, maximum order amount	2	Must	Med

2.3 To show last 5 orders for a customer	2	Could	Med
2.4 To repeat previous order	2	Should	Med
2.5 To default the postage method for a customer depending on order type	2	Won't	High
3. Customers that have not placed an order for 2 years will be archived off the system	1	Could	High
3.1 Customers will be marked as archived for 12 months before being deleted from the system	2	Should	Low
3.2 Customers will be saved to an archive system along with their order history	2	Should	Med

Are these all testable? Yes

Do they go down to enough detail? No

This is where a workshop and further analysis is done to determine the User story for each requirement.

If we look at Requirement 2.3, further details to understand are the business rules to be determined.

Should it be all orders?

What statuses can an order be?

Does it include cancelled orders?

Does it include orders not yet fulfilled?

What about returned orders?

All of these decisions then need to be captured so everyone is clear on what the decision is and how the system will be built.

Once the business requirements are documented there will then be further technical analysis done to determine what data is stored, where is data retrieved from, what size on type of fields will be used, what logic is used, what screens is it seen on. What systems might it need to interface to, to get information from outside of this system. Does this information need to be sent on to another system?

An example of a Business Requirements Document or User story may contain a User flow which looks like this

1. Placing An order on behalf of our customers – Open the Order Screen and Select placing a customer's order.

2. Type the Customers name in the search field and select the required Customer. Alternate Flow- Select Create Customer – User story 2.4.
3. Select the product that the customer wants to order from the drop-down list.
4. Price will be populated when the product is selected.
5. Enter the number of items that the customer wants to order.
6. The total cost will be calculated as the number of items multiplied by price.
7. Select the delivery method requested.
8. If the order qualifies for free delivery (configurable amount – initially set to £100) then cost will be 0.00.
9. If the order doesn't qualify for free delivery the costs is shown and added to the total cost.
10. Select the payment method.
11. If payment method is card, capture the card details and on successful payment, submit the order.
12. If payment method is on account, check the credit limit and submit the order if limit is sufficient, otherwise reject the order.

4 Writing test Cases

If we look at the requirements above, we need to consider what tests we would write to cover these requirements.

If we consider Requirement 1. To be able to place orders on behalf of our customers. Look at each step and assess if it needs to be tested and how it can be tested.

1. Placing An order on behalf of our customers – Open the Order Screen and Select placing a customer's order.

This is just an action as part of a test rather than a test on its own.

2. Type the Customers name in the search field and select the required Customer. Alternate Flow- Select Create Customer – User story 2.4.

Test 1 – Test that you can search for a customer.

Don't forget for every test, consider if there is an opposite. For this test it can be expanded to be –

Test 1 – Test that you can search for a customer that exists and select it from the list.

Test 2 – Test that you can search for a customer that doesn't exist and that you are shown an empty list and a button is available for create customer (Create customer will be tested as part of a different User story)

3. Select the product that the customer wants to order from the drop-down list.

Test 3 – Test that you can select a product and that it is added to your order.

Test 4 – Test that you can add multiple product lines to your order.

Test 5 – Test that you can't add a product that is already on your order.

5 Test Techniques

We have already touched on a few test techniques without realizing it. Requirements Testing is where you write tests from the requirements. This is the Major Technique most used by testers, but to be able to produce better tests it is always good to know of other techniques that give you the greatest coverage of areas more likely to cause issues. Another key one that is underused is Static testing. This is where processes / documents are reviewed or walked through to ensure they are correct before they move on to the next phase.

5.1 Requirements Testing

This is also sometimes referred to as Functional Testing as it tests the individual Functions of a system. Functional testing of a system involves tests that evaluate functions that the system should perform. Functional requirements may be described in work products such as business requirements specifications, epics, user stories, use cases, or functional specifications, or they may be undocumented. The functions are "what" the system should do. Functional tests should be performed at all test levels.

Functional testing considers the behaviour of the software, so it may be used to derive test conditions and test cases for the functionality of the component or system.

5.2 Decision Table Testing

Decision Tables are a concise visual representation for specifying which actions to perform depending on given conditions. They are algorithms whose output is a set of actions. The information expressed in a decision table could also be represented as a decision tree.

Power to circuit	ON		OFF	
Light Switch	ON	OFF	ON	OFF
Bulb glows	Yes	No	No	No

This technique is good to show actual examples where several decisions can be made. It makes it very clear what the parameters are and what the outcomes will be. Producing Tests that match a decision table means that the table can be shared with others for clarification that the requirements are understood. From the table above it is clear that there is a missing requirement to check that the bulb isn't broken as this may also impact the outcome.

5.3 Equivalence Partitioning

Equivalence Partitioning sounds a lot more complicated than it and is probably a technique you have already considered without realising what it is called. It is a technique that divides the input data into partitions of equivalent data from which tests can be derived. In principle, test cases are designed to cover each partition at least once. This technique tries to define test cases that uncover classes of errors, thereby reducing the total number of test cases that must be executed. An advantage of this approach is reduction in the time required for testing software due to lesser number of test cases.

e.g. Postage costs

- up to 1kg - £1,
- over 1kg and up to 10 kg - £2
- up to 50x50x10 add £50p
- over 50x50x10 add £1.50

Weight of parcel	Size of parcel	Expected cost
500g	20x20x5	£1.50
500g	60x60x20	£2.50

2kg	20x20x5	£2.50
2kg	60x60x20	£3.50

5.4 Boundary Value Analysis

Boundary Value Analysis goes hand in hand with Equivalence Partitioning. It is a technique in which tests are designed to include representatives of boundary values in a range. Boundary Value Analysis build on the Equivalence sets as the sets are neighbours, there would exist a boundary between them.

The tests should check on each side of and on the boundary to check for > (greater than) < (less than) and = (equals) as well as >= (greater than and equal to) and <= (less than and equal to) are being processed correctly. There are often software errors at the boundary as the use of > rather than >= may have been used. Looking at the requirements below, it isn't clear if a package of 1kg should be classed in the up to or over category. It should read up to and including 1kg and then over 1kg. Where there is uncertainty, different people can read it to mean different things. Also, the example below misses out 1kg & 50x50x10 which is most likely to be mis interpreted.

e.g. Postage costs

- up to 1kg - £1,

- over 1kg and up to 10 kg - £2
- up to 50x50x10 add £50p
- over 50x50x10 add £1.50

Weight of parcel	Size of parcel	Expected cost
999g	49x49x9	£1.50
1kg	49x49x9	£1.50
1001g	49x49x9	£2.50
9999g	50x50x10	£2.50
10kg	50x50x10	£2.50
10,001g	50x50x10	Error – Too Heavy
999g	51x51x11	£2.50
1kg	51x51x11	£2.50
1001g	51x51x11	£3.50

5.5 Error Guessing

Error guessing is a method in which test cases used to find bugs are established based on experience in prior testing.

The scope of test cases usually relies on the software tester involved, who uses experience and intuition to determine which situations commonly cause software failure. Typical errors include divide by zero, null pointers or invalid parameters. Using your knowledge and experience of your company processes and data means that you might know a customer that places regular large lined orders so might want to include a test that shows the system will cope with the way they order and the size of their statement each month. Also, error guessing can be used when software is used for the first time as issues are more obvious the first time it is used, before you get familiar with the oddities you see.

5.6 State Transition Testing

State transition testing is a type of software testing which is performed to check the change in the state of the application under varying inputs. The condition of input passed is changed and the change in state is observed.

The objective of State Transition testing is:

- To test the behaviour of the system under varying input at differing states.

- To test the dependency on the values in the past.

- To test the change in transition state of the application.

The following diagram shows a state transition diagram that can be used to derive different tests and determine the correct outcome. This not only tests the behaviour of the system through varying inputs but also considers the dependency on values or actions in the past

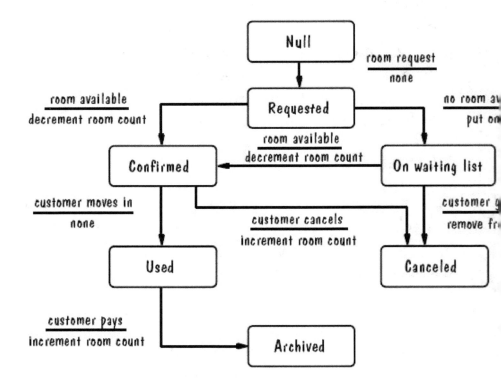

5.7 Use Case Testing

A Use case is a list of actions or event steps typically defining the interactions between a role and a system to achieve a goal. Use cases are a technique to capturing, modelling and specifying the requirements for a system.

Use case diagram.

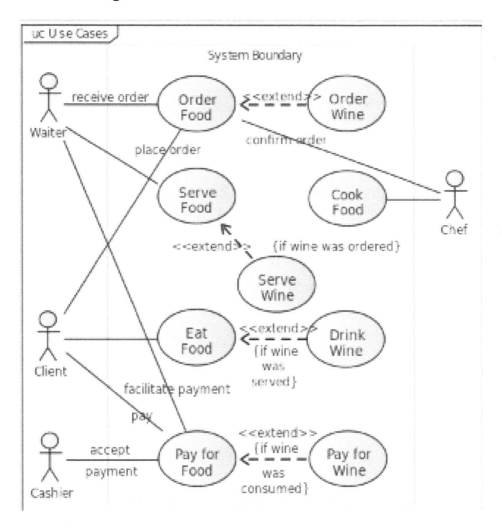

The diagram is usually accompanied by a use case template containing the following sections – Primary

Actor, post conditions, success guarantees, pre-conditions, triggers, basic flow, alternative flows.

Use case testing uses the use case to design test cases and user manuals of the system. There are obvious connections between the flow paths of a use case and the test cases.

5.8 User Story Testing

User Stories are similar to Use cases where they are written for users or customers to influence the functionality of the system based on personas. They usually contain details of acceptance criteria about what the story must do for the product owner to accept it as complete and working as intended. Test cases can then be produced that reflect the story and acceptance criteria.

6 Other Test Phases

As this is a book about UAT I have left other testing phases until the end to give a background on what they are and why there are so many stages of testing.

6.1 Unit Testing

Unit Testing, the first stage of testing,- will be performed on a single, standalone module or unit of code to test basic coding issues and is covered as the code is developed to prove that it works as per approved design and specification. The goal of Unit Testing will be to isolate each component (i.e. individual program, function, procedure, interface mapping etc.) of the application and validate that individual components are working correctly according to its design.

Unit testing should cover:

Database: The application data source supports the requirements of the business in terms of data retrieval.

Functional: Tests that all features and functions of the system comply with those included within the design documents created in the Design phase of the project

Integration: To ensure the system interacts and does not adversely impact the systems it interfaces with. It will also ensure the development of an interfacing module or unit of code meets the requirements of the functional and technical design and is able to: connect to source/target application(s); receive and process a handshake response; and pass/receive data (excluding validating data quality).

6.2 Component Testing / API Testing

This is done by the development team with the testing of individual software components as they are completed, to ensure that the development is functioning according to the design document.

On completion of this test phase, the component(s) should be ready for System Testing or System Integration Testing.

6.3 System Testing

This Test Phase is usually done by a team of System Testers and should be the most rigorous phase of testing as this ensures the functionality of the system is working as it should before the system is handed over by the IT department to customers or users to ensure that the system works with their business processes.

6.4 System Integration Testing

System Integration Testing tests that two systems or components can integrate, talk to each other and also pass the right information to and from each system. Often two systems will talk to each other but may have different formats or codes for their data, e.g. a UK company may use an American website to send orders. The USA website might use a different date format and result in all orders being rejected by the UK system as it thinks the dates are invalid.

Another example is that a company may connect to the Royal Mail system to calculate and pay for postage. The Company system might hold the postage type as 1CL for 1st Class letter post, but this may need to be translated into RML1 for Royal Mail. System Integration Testing also checks responses back from the integrated system to ensure that a good response is returned to ensure that the data or instruction has been received and understood correctly. It may also return further information to allow the sending system to continue with the process e.g. processing a payment may return an authorisation code that confirms that funds are available in the payees bank and the order process can then continue to process the order and approve for dispatch.

6.5 Performance Testing

Performance Testing is used to evaluate the performance of the system in terms of speed, scalability, stability and responsiveness under different workload, either using the maximum number of users at once expected to use the system or the maximum number of transactions per second through several processes. This will measure how the system will deteriorate in terms of the acceptable speed of responses or at what point it will crash. It can also be broken down into types of performance testing including load testing, soak testing, spike testing, stress testing, scalability testing and volume testing.

6.6 Security Testing

Is used to ensure that access to the system is only allowed by those that should be allowed to use it.   It covers hacking of the system by people wanting access to the data to use it for illegal reasons or also ensuring the users of the system also have the necessary access to the areas they should be allowed and no access to the areas they shouldn't have.

6.7 Operational Acceptance Testing

This phase of testing is used to ensure that the implementation of the system works correctly and that all steps are understood before the live implementation is done.   It is often used when there are multiple systems going in at once to ensure that they are all aligned, data is loaded, connections are switched on properly.   It often also includes the roll back plan and reimplementation of the old version of a system to ensure this can be done in the event of a catastrophic failure.

6.8 Usability Testing

Is a phase of testing that looks at usable a system is with real users trying to use it, often while being observed to see where they pause. It can often be done using a tool that captures where the mouse hovers on the screen or AB Testing where half the people see one design and half see an alternative screen. It often looks at how a website looks across different sized devices or how tools to assist with sight impairment work with the screens.

6.9 Regression Testing

Regression Testing is a phase of testing that is used to ensure that changes made to the software do not introduce new bugs or cause existing functionality to break. It is often done after a release of code changes or after go live to confirm that the system is performing as expected. This is the phase that is often automated as it is a set of standard tests that will be run repeatedly so it can reduce the amount of resources required to repeatedly run these tests. It can also give fast results to know if the release has caused any additional issues that need to be investigated.

6.10 Accessibility Testing

Accessibility Testing is a phase of testing that is used to ensure that the software can be used by people with disabilities. It can assist with people who have problems with their sight like blindness, colour blindness, tunnel vision, hearing disabilities or motor control disabilities.

It checks that the software can be used with assistive technology like screen magnification software, braille adaptors, screen reader applications, speech recognition software, specially adapted keyboards for people with motor control disabilities.

7 Finding and Reporting a Bug / Error / Anomaly

You have run your test and the results don't quite look right. What now? Do you just sit and stare at the screen? Doubt yourself as you might have done it wrong? Tell your neighbour that this system is rubbish and you never want to use it again – well you didn't want to use a new system in the first place? Run to your nearest IT person and declare that you have managed to break their system? You can do any of these if you want, but it probably won't get the results you need.

So is it a bug? Is it you? The best thing to do is find out if you were told when you started to be involved in the testing if there is a defect management process for you to report any anomalies. I like to call them anomalies as at the moment we don't know the cause of it, just that something isn't right. This allows someone to investigate it more to see why you have seen this bizarre behaviour (of the system – not you running up to the IT department).

The art of writing a good anomaly report is to know what you did, know what you expect to have happened and what actually happened. If you can add data used and a screenshot as well that would really help.

There is usually a definition of priority and severity of an anomaly to determine if it is a full system outage, a whole area is unusable or if it is just 1 order / account that is impacted. There might also be an assessment of how this issue will impact on the delivery of the project as it may be in an area that needs a 3rd party to fix something.

If it turns out to be an issue with the system, then it will be assigned to a developer to fix and retest before it will be reassigned back to you to retest. This may take several days or weeks so the more information you add, there more it will also assist you with retesting it in the same way you did when you raised it as any deviance may give a different result.

8 Test Tools

There are a wide range of test tools available to help you with your testing. There are always new tools coming on the market so I will name the most popular at the time of writing this. Some will be determined by your company / project as they will be used across multiple test phases / projects and also by the different teams that make up the project. Some tools will combine several functions into one package that can help to assist in a number of areas. If you want to start to use a test tool you should first determine what you want to use it for, what the benefits are you need and how well it fits what you want. Some tools are good for large projects but can add additional time setting it up and maintaining it, so it doesn't give the intended benefit. A tool won't do the job for you and the wrong tool will just make the job harder for you so be sure to choose wisely. Sometimes a spreadsheet and a notepad are just as good a tool for the job.

8.1 Test Management Tools

Test Management tools are used to store test scripts, record execution status of tests, raise and progress defects and report on progress of the testing. There are several tools that cover some or all of these functions. E.g. Jira, Microsoft Azure Dev Ops (ADO), HP Quality Centre, TestRail

8.2 Defect Management Tools

Defect Management Tools are used to create defects reports, assign them through the defect triage and fixing process and then track retesting, release and closure. E.g. Jira, Trello, Assana, MS ADO

8.3 Test Automation Tools

Test Automation Tools are used to automate tests and are often used for regression testing where the same tests are to be run repeatedly for each release. There are several different types of automation tools covering capture & replay of tests, coding of automated tests or simple file comparison tools to compare expected results with actual results. E.g. Selenium, RSAT, Test Grid

8.4 Performance Tools

Performance Testing Tools are used to evaluate the performance of the system in terms of speed, scalability, stability and responsiveness under different workloads. E.G. Apache JMeter, BrowserStack, Load Runner

8.5 Cross Browser Test Tools

Cross Browser Test Tools are used to emulate a website or application viewed on a number of different browsers, devices and screen sizes. E.g. Browser Stack, Testgrid, Applitools eyes, Autify

8.6 Mobile Emulator Test Tools

The Mobile Emulators allow you to run your phone Application on your PC. This helps with initial testing as it is quicker and easier to use a PC. The down side to mobile emulators is that they don't always behave in the same way as a mobile device, so you also need to use the actual device as part of your testing. E.g. Android Studio, Appetize, iPadian

8.7 Usability Test Tools

Usability Test Tools monitor how users experience your application. E.g. Maze, Hotjar, Userfeel

8.8 Test Data Generator

A Test Data Generator is used to generate large amounts of data for testing, quickly to save having to run numerous processes manually. E.G. Mockaroo, SQL Data Generator, Jmeter,

8.9 API Test Tools

APIs are Application Programming Interfaces which is where two different applications communicate with each other. The test tools are used to mimic one of the applications calling an interfaces on the other application. They can be used in place of having a full end to end environment or to call a program with parameters that

might not be used to force specific errors. E.g Postman,
Soap UI

9 The Half an Hour Test

The Half an hour test can be used in a number of situations to give a good feedback over a short period of testing.

9.1 First pass of testing

When software is first delivered in the first phase of UAT or a new sprint delivery, the first half an hour is vital as you see it for the first time with new eyes. You look at it without glancing over things you have already seen that are wrong as you are looking for new things so spot things you won't see next time. Make note of all the things you spot that you want to come back to later as you will forget them and may not see them next time. Just a quick note and move on to explore more.

9.2 Regression Testing

If you only have half an hour to test the system, what would you want / need to cover first? This can be handy to have a quick tick list to use when a new version is deployed, just to make sure before you move on that you are happy that the deployment has worked and not broken the main areas you will need.

9.3 Post Go Live Smoke Testing

When a system has gone live it is useful to know it is working in the same way it worked in the test environment. It often isn't possible to perform the same tasks in a live environment that you could in a test environment as you don't want to make payments, place orders or archive data, so again it is handy to have a tick list of areas you would want to check that are highest priority.

10 Risk Based Testing

What is Risk Based Testing? It is obviously testing the areas of highest risk. But how do you know what they are? One way of defining this is to look at the likelihoods and impacts of something happening and compare it to other processes risk score.

An example of this could be making payments on a website or producing a report of repeat customers. You can define your own risk areas as long as you score the items on the same categories. Scores – 1 = Very Low, 5- Medium, 9 – Very High

Likelihood of issue		
	Make a payment	Report of repeat customers
Complexity of code	9	3
Technology	7	3
Interfaces	7	1
Reuse of code	9	1
Size of code	7	3
Total	39	11

Impact of issue		
	Make a payment	Report of repeat customers
Financial	9	5
User Importance	9	1
Security	9	5
Performance	7	1
Usage	9	3
Total	**36**	**15**

So, from the above results you can see that making a payment is much higher risk than the report. This shows that more time should be spent on testing the payments to reduce the risk of something going wrong when the code goes live.

You can set your own categories and define them to suit your business area. For different companies and departments, financial impact might mean different things – loss of orders, cost of paying fines, cost of resources to work on the area to fix issues.

11 Testing Environments

Testing environments are areas where the code and data is deployed ready for testing to take place. This can be a complete copy of the live system with all connecting systems in place or may be a cut down version with a percentage of the data and only some if any connections. Often 3rd party companies will only make 1 test system available to their customers so there needs to be consideration around whether you can connect multiple environments to their test system.

Often Test environments will have names that relate to the test phases so it is clear what the flow of code movement to production is, but sometimes, test phases can be performed in different environments. e.g. UAT Test phase could take place in a SIT Test environment if another project is using the UAT environment and is close to going live and doesn't want new code being put in the environment.

Sometimes test environments are built fresh for a new project if it is a new system, or they might be an ongoing environment that is allocated for the project. You need to be aware of what other testing is ongoing in that environment or code releases that will be happening during your test Phase as this could impact on your expected results.

There should be a diagram available for you to see showing the layout of the test environment and all connected systems.

www.ingramcontent.com/pod-product-compliance
Lightning Source LLC
LaVergne TN
LVHW051632050326
832903LV00033B/4721